ROYAL COURT

G000075002

Royal Court Theatre presents

THE ELEVENTH CAPITAL

by **Alexandra Wood**

First performance at the Royal Court Jerwood Theatre Upstairs, Sloane Square, London on 23 February 2007.

The Young Writers Festival is supported by
John Lyon's Charity
Columbia Foundation
The Foyle Foundation

THE ELEVENTH CAPITAL

by **Alexandra Wood**

Cast in order of appearance
Neighbour/Woman **Emily Joyce**
Cleaner/Journalist **Rebekah Staton**
Thief 1/Carpenter **Emil Marwa**
Thief 2/Driver **John Hodgkinson**
Civil Servant 1/Entrepreneur **Karl Collins**
Civil Servant 2 **Ryan Early**
Girl **Charlene McKenna**
Boy **David Judge**

Director **Natalie Abrahami**
Designer **James Cotterill**
Lighting Designer **Greg Gould**
Sound Designer **Ian Dickinson**
Composer **Keith Clouston**
Assistant Director **David Mercatali**
Casting **Amy Ball**
Production Manager **Sue Bird**
Stage Managers **Amy Almond, Catherine Lockett**
Stage Management Work Placement **Bonnie Morris**
Costume Supervisor **Jackie Orton**

The Royal Court Theatre would like to thank Stuart Kimber, Friendly Drinks and Darren Elliott for supporting the Writers' Receptions.

Thanks to: Steve Atkinson, Humphrey Barber, Esther Baker, Richard Bean, Suzanne Bell, Amy Belson, Simon Bennett, Jane Bodie, Simon Bowen, Indi Boyd Maunsell, Linda Brogan, Sean Buckley, Sarah Cattle, Anna Coombs, Hall for Cornwall, Karen Dainty, Kirstie Davis, David Dipper, Jackie Downs, Shehani Fernando, Mel Halsall, Layne Harrod, Andrew Haydon, Paula Henstock, Anna Holmfield, Richard Hurst, Lucy Kerbel, Dawn King, Nicholai Labarrie, Nigel Linzertorte-Smythe, Aoife Mannix, Elina Manni, Sara Masters, Clare McQuillan, Will Mortimer, Sue Mayo, Pip Minnithrorpe, Claire Newlove, Leann O'Kasi, Rachel Parish, Sylvia Paskin, George Perrin, Marissa Phillips, Paul Robinson, Nicola Sangster, Katy Silverton, Lisa Spirling, Sally Stott, Gareth Tudor Price, Hull Truck Theatre Co, Lyndsey Turner, Simon Vinnicombe, Ian Wainwright, Dawn Walton, Watford Palace Theatre, Tiffany Watt-Smith and Sheila White.

Special thanks to Caryn Stanley.

THE COMPANY

Alexandra Wood (writer)

Alexandra took part in YWP introductory and advanced writers' groups in 2006. She is the Literary Manager at Finborough Theatre. This is her first professionally produced play.

Natalie Abrahami (director)

For the Royal Court, as director: Love is Blind (International Residency), The Grace of Mary Traverse (reading), From Here to the Moon (reading).

For the Royal Court, as assistant director: Fallout, Caryl Churchill Shorts Season.

Other theatre as director includes: The Seagull (Oxford School of Drama); Candleford (Oxfordshire Museum); Play and Not I (BAC); Human Rites (Southwark Playhouse).

Other theatre as assistant director includes: Watership Down (Lyric Hammersmith); Measure for Measure (National); The Storm, The Tempest (Globe); The Anniversary (Liverpool Playhouse); The Mercy Seat (Almeida).

Awards: 2005 James Menzies-Kitchin Award for Directors for Play and Not I.

Natalie has recently been appointed joint Artistic Director of The Gate.

Keith Clouston (composer)

As composer, theatre includes: Magic Carpet (Lyric Hammersmith); Tamburlaine (Bristol Old Vic/Barbican); The UN Inspector (National); Julius Caesar (RSC/national tour & USA/Lyric Hammersmith); Coriolanus (RSC/national tour & USA /Old Vic); A Midsummer Night's Dream, Comedy of Errors, Paradise Lost, Twelfth Night (Bristol Old Vic); Night of the Soul (RSC Barbican); The Women of Troy (RADA); Death of a Salesman (Compass Touring); Electra, Trojan Women (Cambridge Greek Play, Cambridge Arts).

As composer film includes: Mothercare (Raindance Festival).

Other composition includes: Tears for string orchestra (Spitalfields Festival/Royal Academy of Music); Songs, improvisations and compositions (ICA).

As musician, theatre includes: Peer Gynt (National); The Comedy of Errors (RSC/tour/ Young Vic); The Comedy of Errors (Globe).

As musician television and radio includes: Later with Jools Holland, The Girlie Show,

Painted Lady, The Life of Mohammed, Glastonbury '99, The Bill, The Andy Kershaw Show, Loose Ends, Antony and Cleopatra, The Iliad.

As musician film includes: Beloved.

Live performance includes: Speaking in Tongues (ICA); Natacha Atlas (Queen Elizabeth Hall/ WOMAD/Glastonbury Festival/Brazil/Europe/ USA); MIRA Ensemble (Montreux Jazz Festival); Cheb Mami (Olympia, Paris); Hakim (Marseilles Festival); David Arnold (Shepherds Bush Empire).

Karl Collins

Theatre includes: Fabulation, Darfur Plays (Tricycle); The Measles (Gate); The Meeting (Riverside); Borders of Paradise (Palace, Watford); King Lear (tour/Cochrane); Statements After an Arrest (Arts Threshold Theatre); Fuente Ovejuna (National); Sarita (National Theatre Studio); The Beggar's Opera (Belgrade Theatre); Things Past (London/Hong Kong); The Guise (Romania/Hong Kong/ Boston/New York).

Television includes: New Street Law, 55 Degrees North, A Thing Called Love, Grease Monkeys, The Bill, Metrosexuality.

Film includes: Life and Lyrics, The Booth, Greenwich Mean Time, Twentyfourseven, Robert Ryland's Last Journey.

James Cotterill (designer)

For the Royal Court: Gone Too Far!

Other theatre includes: Big Sale (The Place); Fair (Trafalgar Studios); Silverland, 15 Minutes (Arcola); Widows, The Fool (RADA); The Gabriels (Finborough).

Awards include: 2005 Linbury Prize for Stage Design for Not the End of the World (Bristol Old Vic).

Ian Dickinson (sound designer)

For the Royal Court: The Seagull, Krapp's Last Tape, Piano/Forte, Rock 'n' Roll (& Duke of York's), Motortown, Rainbow Kiss, The Winterling, Alice Trilogy, Fewer Emergencies, Way to Heaven, The Woman Before, Stoning Mary (& Drum Theatre, Plymouth), Breathing Corpses, Wild East, Dumb Show, Shining City (& Gate, Dublin), Lucky Dog, Blest Be the Tie (with Talawa), Ladybird, Notes on Falling Leaves, Loyal Women, The Sugar Syndrome, Blood, Playing the Victim (with Told By an Idiot), Fallout, Flesh Wound, Hitchcock Blonde (& Lyric), Black Milk, Crazyblackmuthafuckin'self, Caryl Churchill Shorts, Push Up, Fucking Games, Herons.

Other theatre includes: King Of Hearts (Out of Joint); Love and Money (Young Vic); Much Ado About Nothing (redesign, RSC/Novello); Pillars of the Community (National); A Few Good Men (Haymarket); Dr Faustus (Chichester Festival Theatre); The Magic Carpet (Lyric Hammersmith); Port, As You Like It, Poor Superman, Martin Yesterday, Fast Food, Coyote Ugly (Royal Exchange, Manchester); Night of the Soul (RSC/Barbican); Eyes of the Kappa (Gate); Crime & Punishment in Dalston (Arcola); Search & Destroy (New End); The Whore's Dream (RSC/Edinburgh).

Ian is Head of Sound at the Royal Court.

Ryan Early

Theatre includes: Beau Brummell (59E59 Theater, New York); The Knight of the Burning Pestle (Barbican); Miss Yesterday (Stephen Joseph, Scarborough); The Country Wife (Palace, Watford); About Face (Almeida Studio); Oliver Twist, The Servant (Lyric Hammersmith); A Midsummer Night's Dream, The Golden Ass (Globe); Spring and Port Wine (West Yorkshire Playhouse); The Secret Garden (Nottingham Playhouse); One Life and Counting (Bush/Channel 4).

Television includes: Doctors, Love Soup, Heartbeat, The Bill, The Detective, Soup.

Film includes: Besame Mucho, The Slot, An Acre of Moon.

Radio includes: Maths Man, Words for You.

Greg Gould (lighting designer)

Theatre includes: A Room of One's Own, Snowbull (Hampstead); Two Clouds Over Eden, Jerusalem Syndrome (Royal Exchange, Manchester).

Greg is Lighting Deputy at the Royal Court.

John Hodgkinson

Theatre includes: The Taming of the Shrew, A Midsummer Night's Dream, The Two Gentlemen of Verona, Romeo and Juliet, As You Like It, Oh What a Lovely War (Regent's Park); A Journey to London (Orange Tree); Neville's Island, The Hare Trilogy: Racing Demon, Absence of War, Murmuring Judges (Birmingham Rep.); I Have Been Here Before (Watford Palace); Arcadia

(BOV); Alice in Wonderland, Love's Labours Lost, A Jovial Crew, The Beggar's Opera, The Winter's Tale, Dr Jekyll & Mr Hyde, The Pretenders, Richard II, Edward II, The Comedy of Errors, Events Whilst Guarding the Bofor's Gun (RSC); The Front Page (Donmar); Le Bourgeois Gentilhomme (Edinburgh Festival); The Visit (Chichester); The Seagull (National); London Assurance (Chichester/West End); Love's Labours Lost (Chichester); Cardboard City (Soho Poly/tour).

Television includes: Heartbeat, Broken News, Doctors, Brief Encounters, Peep Show, East Enders, My Family, The Lee Evans Show, Holby City, Chambers, The Bill, The Estate Agents, People Like Us, Kiss Me Kate, The Peter Principle, Pure Wickedness, Boyz Unlimited, Then, Keeping Mum, Duck Patrol, Dad, Sometime Never, Inside Victor Lewis Smith.

Film includes: Thunderpants, Firelight, Whatever Happened to Harold Smith.

Emily Joyce

For the Royal Court: Stoning Mary.

Other theatre includes: 50 Revolutions (Whitehall); Twelfth Night, A Christmas Carol, Love's Labours Lost, King Baby, 'Tis Pity She's a Whore, Romeo and Juliet (RSC); Hayfever, Charley's Aunt (Northcott, Exeter); Romeo and Juliet (Ipswich).

Television includes: Dalziel & Pascoe, My Mum and Dad Are at It, Hotel Babylon, My Hero, Ultimate Force, Inspector Lynley Mysteries, Messiah II, Midsomer Murders, The Glass, Hero of the Hour, Trial by Fire, Grafters, In Exile, Jane Eyre, Cracker, Casualty.

Film includes: The Woodlanders.

David Judge

Theatre includes: The Rise and Fall of Little Voice (Harrogate); Christmas is Miles Away (Royal Exchange Manchester/Bush); Afterbirth (Arcola); A Taste of Honey (North Face Theatre Co./Royal Northern College of Music); Irish Pelè (Contact).

Television includes: Doctors, New Street Law, Silent Witness, Casualty.

Film includes: American Haunting.

Emil Marwa

For the Royal Court: East is East (Royal Court/Tamasha/Birmingham Rep co-production).

Other theatre includes: Hijra (Bush/Plymouth);
All's Well That Ends Well (Oxford Stage Co.);
Simple Past (Gate); Gift (White Bear); Gum &
Goo (Bird's Nest).
Television includes: Trevor Island, Murphy's
Law, Banglatown Banquet, Hustle, Holby City,
Waking the Dead, The Grid, Passer By,
No Angels, Dalziel & Pascoe, Real Men,
Bodily Harm, Stan the Man, Casualty,
City Central, Dangerfield, Out of Hours,
East Enders, Grange Hill.
Film includes: Friends and Enemies, Izatt,
Code 46, Death of Klinghoffer, The Guru,
Club le Monde, East is East, The Last Yellow,
The Darkest Light, Sari and Trainers,
Uncle Harry's, Sandwich, Textual Attraction,
Four Brothers and a Funeral.

Charlene McKenna
Theatre includes: One of These Days (RSC);
Lonesome West (Lyric, Belfast); Romeo and
Juliet, Feelin' Strangely Fine, Slice of Saturday
Night, Little Shop of Horrors, Dancing at
Lughnasa (The Garage, Monaghan).
Television includes: Kitchen, 99-100, Pure Mule,
Ghost Stories.
Film includes: Tiger's Tale, Breakfast on Pluto,
Redemption for Brent, Social Work,
Middletown, Small Engine Repair, Eighteenth
Electricity Plan.

David Mercatali (assistant director)
As director, theatre includes: !Runners – The
Return (Edinburgh Festival); Paint Over
(Blue Elephant); The Birthday Party
(Quaker Meeting House); Death of a Salesman
(Sherman).
As assistant director, theatre includes:
Funny Money (Shangri La Hotel); Powerless
(Baron's Court); Waking Up Suddenly, !Runners
(Blue Elephant).

Rebekah Staton
Theatre includes: Playing with Fire (National);
The Crucible (Crucible); Simplicity, Chasing the
Golden Sun (Orange Tree).
Film and television includes: Dr Who,
Confessions of a Diary Secretary, Pulling,
The Amazing Mrs Pritchard, Rome, Mysterious
Creatures, Jane Eyre, Golden Hour, The Brief,
Jericho, Outlaws, Life Begins, State of Play,
Bright Young Things.
Radio includes: Woman's Hour.

THE ENGLISH STAGE COMPANY AT THE ROYAL COURT

The English Stage Company at the Royal Court opened in 1956 as a subsidised theatre producing new British plays, international plays and some classical revivals.

The first artistic director George Devine aimed to create a writers' theatre, 'a place where the dramatist is acknowledged as the fundamental creative force in the theatre and where the play is more important than the actors, the director, the designer'. The urgent need was to find a contemporary style in which the play, the acting, direction and design are all combined. He believed that 'the battle will be a long one to continue to create the right conditions for writers to work in'.

Devine aimed to discover 'hard-hitting, uncompromising writers whose plays are stimulating, provocative and exciting'. The Royal Court production of John Osborne's Look Back in Anger in May 1956 is now seen as the decisive starting point of modern British drama and the policy created a new generation of British playwrights. The first wave included John Osborne, Arnold Wesker, John Arden, Ann Jellicoe, N F Simpson and Edward Bond. Early seasons included new international plays by Bertolt Brecht, Eugène Ionesco, Samuel Beckett and Jean-Paul Sartre.

The theatre started with the 400-seat proscenium arch Theatre Downstairs, and in 1969 opened a second theatre, the 60-seat studio Theatre Upstairs. Some productions transfer to the West End, such as Tom Stoppard's Rock 'n' Roll, My Name is Rachel Corrie, Terry Johnson's Hitchcock Blonde, Caryl Churchill's Far Away and Conor McPherson's The Weir. Recent touring productions include Sarah Kane's 4.48 Psychosis (US tour) and Ché Walker's Flesh Wound (Galway Arts Festival). The Royal Court also co-produces plays which transfer to the West End or tour internationally, such as Conor McPherson's Shining City (with Gate Theatre, Dublin), Sebastian Barry's The Steward of Christendom and Mark Ravenhill's Shopping and Fucking (with Out of Joint), Martin McDonagh's The Beauty Queen Of Leenane (with Druid), Ayub Khan Din's East is East (with Tamasha).

Since 1994 the Royal Court's artistic policy has again been vigorously directed to finding and producing a new generation of playwrights. The writers include Joe Penhall, Rebecca Prichard, Michael Wynne, Nick Grosso, Judy Upton, Meredith Oakes, Sarah Kane, Anthony Neilson, Judith Johnson, James Stock, Jez Butterworth, Marina Carr, Phyllis Nagy, Simon Block, Martin McDonagh, Mark Ravenhill, Ayub Khan Din, Tamantha Hammerschlag,

photo: Stephen Cummiiskey

Jess Walters, Ché Walker, Conor McPherson, Simon Stephens, Richard Bean, Roy Williams, Gary Mitchell, Mick Mahoney, Rebecca Gilman, Christopher Shinn, Kia Corthron, David Gieselmann, Marius von Mayenburg, David Eldridge, Leo Butler, Zinnie Harris, Grae Cleugh, Roland Schimmelpfennig, Chloe Moss, DeObia Oparei, Enda Walsh, Vassily Sigarev, the Presnyakov Brothers, Marcos Barbosa, Lucy Prebble, John Donnelly, Clare Pollard, Robin French, Elyzabeth Gregory Wilder, Rob Evans, Laura Wade, Debbie Tucker Green, Levi David Addai and Simon Farquhar. This expanded programme of new plays has been made possible through the support of A.S.K. Theater Projects and the Skirball Foundation, The Jerwood Charity, the American Friends of the Royal Court Theatre and (in 1994/5 and 1999) the National Theatre Studio.

The refurbished theatre in Sloane Square opened in February 2000, with a policy still inspired by the first artistic director George Devine. The Royal Court is an international theatre for new plays and new playwrights, and the work shapes contemporary drama in Britain and overseas.

The Royal Court's long and successful history of innovation has been built by generations of gifted and imaginative individuals. For information on the many exciting ways you can help support the theatre, please contact the Development Department on 020 7565 5079.

AWARDS FOR
THE ROYAL COURT

Martin McDonagh won the 1996 George Devine Award, the 1996 Writers' Guild Best Fringe Play Award, the 1996 Critics' Circle Award and the 1996 Evening Standard Award for Most Promising Playwright for The Beauty Queen of Leenane. Marina Carr won the 19th Susan Smith Blackburn Prize (1996/7) for Portia Coughlan. Conor McPherson won the 1997 George Devine Award, the 1997 Critics' Circle Award and the 1997 Evening Standard Award for Most Promising Playwright for The Weir. Ayub Khan Din won the 1997 Writers' Guild Awards for Best West End Play and New Writer of the Year and the 1996 John Whiting Award for East is East (co-production with Tamasha).

Martin McDonagh's The Beauty Queen of Leenane (co-production with Druid Theatre Company) won four 1998 Tony Awards including Garry Hynes for Best Director. Eugene Ionesco's The Chairs (co-production with Theatre de Complicite) was nominated for six Tony awards. David Hare won the 1998 Time Out Live Award for Outstanding Achievement and six awards in New York including the Drama League, Drama Desk and New York Critics Circle Award for Via Dolorosa. Sarah Kane won the 1998 Arts Foundation Fellowship in Playwriting. Rebecca Prichard won the 1998 Critics' Circle Award for Most Promising Playwright for Yard Gal (co-production with Clean Break).

Conor McPherson won the 1999 Olivier Award for Best New Play for The Weir. The Royal Court won the 1999 ITI Award for Excellence in International Theatre. Sarah Kane's Cleansed was judged Best Foreign Language Play in 1999 by Theater Heute in Germany. Gary Mitchell won the 1999 Pearson Best Play Award for Trust. Rebecca Gilman was joint winner of the 1999 George Devine Award and won the 1999 Evening Standard Award for Most Promising Playwright for The Glory of Living.

In 1999, the Royal Court won the European theatre prize New Theatrical Realities, presented at Taormina Arte in Sicily, for its efforts in recent years in discovering and producing the work of young British dramatists.

Roy Williams and Gary Mitchell were joint winners of the George Devine Award 2000 for Most Promising Playwright for Lift Off and The Force of Change respectively. At the Barclays Theatre Awards 2000 presented by the TMA, Richard Wilson won the Best Director Award for David Gieselmann's Mr Kolpert and Jeremy Herbert won the Best Designer Award for Sarah Kane's 4.48 Psychosis. Gary Mitchell won the Evening Standard's Charles Wintour Award 2000 for Most Promising Playwright for The Force of Change. Stephen Jeffreys' I Just Stopped by to See the Man won an AT&T: On Stage Award 2000.

David Eldridge's Under the Blue Sky won the Time Out Live Award 2001 for Best New Play in the West End. Leo Butler won the George Devine Award 2001 for Most Promising Playwright for Redundant. Roy Williams won the Evening Standard's Charles Wintour Award 2001 for Most Promising Playwright for Clubland. Grae Cleugh won the 2001 Olivier Award for Most Promising Playwright for Fucking Games.

Richard Bean was joint winner of the George Devine Award 2002 for Most Promising Playwright for Under the Whaleback. Caryl Churchill won the 2002 Evening Standard Award for Best New Play for A Number. Vassily Sigarev won the 2002 Evening Standard Charles Wintour Award for Most Promising Playwright for Plasticine. Ian MacNeil won the 2002 Evening Standard Award for Best Design for A Number and Plasticine. Peter Gill won the 2002 Critics' Circle Award for Best New Play for The York Realist (English Touring Theatre). Ché Walker won the 2003 George Devine Award for Most Promising Playwright for Flesh Wound. Lucy Prebble won the 2003 Critics' Circle Award and the 2004 George Devine Award for Most Promising Playwright, and the TMA Theatre Award 2004 for Best New Play for The Sugar Syndrome. Richard Bean won the 2005 Critics' Circle Award for Best New Play for Harvest. Laura Wade won the 2005 Critics' Circle Award for Most Promising Playwright and the 2005 Pearson Best Play Award for Breathing Corpses. The 2006 Whatsonstage Theatregoers' Choice Award for Best New Play was won by My Name is Rachel Corrie. The 2005 Evening Standard Special Award was given to the Royal Court 'for making and changing theatrical history this last half century'.

Tom Stoppard's Rock 'n' Roll won the 2006 Evening Standard Award for Best Play and the 2006 Critics' Circle Award for Best Play.

ROYAL COURT BOOKSHOP

The Royal Court bookshop offers a range of contemporary plays and publications on the theory and practice of modern drama. The staff specialise in assisting with the selection of audition monologues and scenes. Royal Court playtexts from past and present productions cost £2.
The Bookshop is situated to the right of the stairs leading to the ROYAL COURT CAFE BAR.

Monday to Friday 3 – 10pm
Saturday 2.30 – 10pm
(Closed shortly every evening from 7.45 to 8.15pm)

For information tel: 020 7565 5024
or email: bookshop@royalcourttheatre.com

Books can also be ordered from our website
www.royalcourttheatre.com

PROGRAMME SUPPORTERS

The Royal Court (English Stage Company Ltd) receives its principal funding from Arts Council England, London. It is also supported financially by a wide range of private companies, charitable and public bodies, and earns the remainder of its income from the box office and its own trading activities.

The Genesis Foundation supports the Royal Court's work with International Playwrights.

The Artistic Director's Chair is supported by a lead grant from The Peter Jay Sharp Foundation, contributing to the activities of the Artistic Director's office. Over the past nine years the BBC has supported the Gerald Chapman Fund for directors.

Archival recordings of the Royal Court's Anniversary year were made possible by Francis Finlay.

THE AMERICAN FRIENDS OF THE ROYAL COURT THEATRE

AFRCT supports the mission of the Royal Court and are primarily focused on raising funds to enable the theatre to produce new work by emerging American writers. Since this not-for-profit organisation was founded in 1997, AFRCT has contributed to ten productions. It has also supported the participation of young artists in the Royal Court's acclaimed International Residency.

ROYAL COURT

14 March – 7 April
Jerwood Theatre Upstairs

A Royal Court Theatre and Druid co-production

LEAVES

by Lucy Caldwell

direction **Garry Hynes**

"We are where we come from?" That's not true. That's not true because if that's true there's no hope for any of us.

Lori is coming home from her first term at university. It's only been a few weeks and already things have gone badly wrong. But none of the rest of the family knows, or understands, what really happened.

In this fiercely observed family drama, three teenage girls struggle to define who they are, and why, and where they might be going.

Leaves won the George Devine Award 2006, the premier award for new writing by an emerging playwright.

28 March – 21 April
Jerwood Theatre Downstairs

A National Theatre of Scotland production

THE WONDERFUL WORLD OF DISSOCIA

by Anthony Neilson

direction **Anthony Neilson**

Lisa Jones is on a journey. It's a colourful and exciting off-kilter trip in search of one lost hour that has tipped the balance of her life. The inhabitants of the wonderful world she finds herself in – Dissocia – are a curious blend of the funny, the friendly and the brutal. As Neilson himself puts it, 'If you like Alice in Wonderland but there's not enough sex and violence in it, then Dissocia is the show for you'.

Produced originally for the 2004 Edinburgh International Festival, The Wonderful World of Dissocia wowed critics and audiences alike.

This is a hugely original play, both magical and moving, that confirmed Anthony Neilson as one of the major voices in contemporary British theatre.

BOX OFFICE 020 7565 5000
BOOK ONLINE
www.royalcourttheatre.com

THE ELEVENTH CAPITAL

Alexandra Wood

For Mum, Dad,
Rachel and Alistair

Thanks

I'd like to thank Neil for pointing me in the direction
of Burma, Leo and the rest of the YWP team
for their support and enthusiasm,
Sacha for her guidance with rewriting, and
Lee for her sensitive and imaginative approach
to the play.

AW

4

Characters
in order of appearance

NEIGHBOUR

CLEANER

THIEF 1

THIEF 2

CIVIL SERVANT 1

CIVIL SERVANT 2

ENTREPRENEUR

CARPENTER

JOURNALIST

GIRL

BOY

WOMAN

DRIVER

Actors may play multiple parts when necessary.

Note

A forward slash (/) marks the point where one character interrupts the other.

Scene One

Early evening, the sun has almost set. The NEIGHBOUR *is tending to her modest garden before the light goes. The* CLEANER *arrives home.*

NEIGHBOUR. You only just getting home?

CLEANER. Yes.

NEIGHBOUR. It's a long day is all I meant.

CLEANER. I'm not afraid of a bit of hard work.

NEIGHBOUR. No, of course not, that's not . . .

Pause.

CLEANER. You want to be careful.

NEIGHBOUR. Oh?

CLEANER (*indicating the plants*). Not to overdo it with the pruning.

NEIGHBOUR. Oh yes. Thank you.

CLEANER. You spend a lot of time out here.

NEIGHBOUR. Yes, I like my garden.

CLEANER. You didn't used to.

NEIGHBOUR. I always loved it.

CLEANER. It seems more of a recent thing.

NEIGHBOUR. I just didn't have the time before, but since the children have grown up a little I can do a few things I used to like doing.

CLEANER. It'd be nice to have the time.

NEIGHBOUR. You will. When the girls are a little older you'll find you can reclaim your life!

CLEANER. They haven't stolen it.

NEIGHBOUR. No, of course not, but children are time-consuming, that's all.

CLEANER. Well, they're also essential to the future of the nation, so until we come up with a less time-consuming alternative, I guess we'll all have to deal with a little less gardening.

NEIGHBOUR. Oh for . . . Look, I won't keep you, you'll want to get in and see the girls. It's been a long day for you.

Pause.

CLEANER. Yes, I've been given extra responsibilities at work.

NEIGHBOUR. Congratulations.

CLEANER. Thank you.

NEIGHBOUR. An honour.

CLEANER. Yes, I'm in the offices now.

NEIGHBOUR. You didn't mention . . . when did this happen?

CLEANER. It's not something I'm supposed to talk about.

NEIGHBOUR. Of course not, / I understand.

CLEANER. A few weeks ago. That's probably all I can say.

NEIGHBOUR. I've heard the offices are . . . magnificent.

CLEANER. I do my best to keep them that way.

NEIGHBOUR. Lots of marble. That's what I've heard.

CLEANER. I can't really / reveal

NEIGHBOUR. It seems a shame they should be moving.

CLEANER. All I'll say, is that I do spend a fair amount of time polishing.

NEIGHBOUR. An honour.

CLEANER. Of course. And I was in one of the directors' offices today.

NEIGHBOUR. A privilege.

CLEANER. Yes. I was only cleaning, but people do walk in and out, carry on as normal, like I'm not there. And I'm discreet of course, just get on with my business.

NEIGHBOUR. Of polishing the marble.

CLEANER. Of polishing, yes.

NEIGHBOUR. They must trust you.

CLEANER. They've no reason not to.

NEIGHBOUR. No.

Pause.

CLEANER. I've seen the Commander, you know.

NEIGHBOUR. What was he doing?

CLEANER. He was walking down the corridor, while I was washing the walls.

NEIGHBOUR. I saw him at an Armed Forces Day rally. He looked small, but then, I was quite far away.

CLEANER. He's average size when you're up close, I'd say. But when he walked past me, even though I was facing the other way, I knew it was him.

NEIGHBOUR. You were facing the other way?

CLEANER. I was washing the walls. You think it wasn't him?

NEIGHBOUR. I'm sure it was.

CLEANER. I'm telling you it was, if you'd been that close, you'd know there's no mistaking him.

NEIGHBOUR. It's an honour.

CLEANER. Exactly.

NEIGHBOUR. Far more glamorous than my classroom, I'm sure.

CLEANER. Yes, I overheard a man try to resign today.

NEIGHBOUR. A privilege.

CLEANER. Yes. When you're working in a director's office, you hear these things all the time.

NEIGHBOUR. So he's an important director?

CLEANER. Seems to be. Yes, he is. But you can't let that affect you, I just get on with my job, you have to be professional.

NEIGHBOUR. I know. I tutored the children of one of the directors a while ago, and you just have to keep your head down, stick to the curriculum.

CLEANER. You don't tutor them any more?

NEIGHBOUR. They moved away.

CLEANER. As long as it wasn't that you strayed from the curriculum. (*She laughs.*)

NEIGHBOUR (*laughs*). No, they moved.

CLEANER. That's why the man today was trying to resign.

NEIGHBOUR. He's being moved too?

CLEANER. I guess so.

NEIGHBOUR. To the new capital?

CLEANER. Well, it won't build itself.

Pause.

I've never seen a man sweat so much. He came in leaving a trail across the floor like some wet animal.

NEIGHBOUR. Marble's dangerous when it gets wet.

CLEANER. I'd just cleaned the floor as well.

NEIGHBOUR. He probably wasn't doing it to spite you.

CLEANER. After they shook hands I heard the director dry his hand on his trousers.

NEIGHBOUR. You heard that?

CLEANER. There was no other sound.

NEIGHBOUR. You didn't turn to look?

CLEANER. I've told you, it's no business of mine, I'm no spy, I just get on with my job.

NEIGHBOUR. Of course, sorry.

CLEANER. You're asking a lot of questions.

NEIGHBOUR. You're right, sorry.

CLEANER. How are the family? Everyone well?

NEIGHBOUR. Well? Yes, everyone's fine.

CLEANER. That's what the director said to the man.

NEIGHBOUR. Oh.

CLEANER. The wife and boys? Everyone well?

NEIGHBOUR. Bit of an ice-breaker.

CLEANER. Exactly. He always asks, helps relax them.

NEIGHBOUR. Did it help this man?

CLEANER. I don't know. He continued to sweat.

NEIGHBOUR. Might have a medical condition.

CLEANER. I'm afraid it's not possible. I don't accept your resignation. It was as simple as that.

NEIGHBOUR. No more small talk?

CLEANER. Directors don't need to explain.

NEIGHBOUR. Of course not.

CLEANER. And why should he want to resign anyway? It doesn't make sense. He's obviously in a good job.

NEIGHBOUR. He has to leave his family?

CLEANER. Only for a while. They'll be able to join him soon. Once there's a city.

NEIGHBOUR. A water supply, houses, that kind of thing?

CLEANER. Would you have them go without?

NEIGHBOUR. The father of one of the girls at school is having to go.

CLEANER. In my position, I hear of men every day having to go.

NEIGHBOUR. I'm sure.

CLEANER. In the offices, where I am, you get used to it.

NEIGHBOUR. I don't think I could get used to the idea of leaving my children.

CLEANER. And you think I could?

Pause.

NEIGHBOUR. I'll let you go in and see your girls, they must miss you.

CLEANER. Why would they miss me?

NEIGHBOUR. I just meant, with your longer hours, they / must

CLEANER. I'm back at the end of the day, aren't I?

NEIGHBOUR. Yes, you are.

Pause.

CLEANER. He begged for a while. I listened to him beg. I couldn't tell if he was crying, whether it was the tears or the sweat that was hitting the floor. It could've been tears.

NEIGHBOUR. Making the marble wet.

CLEANER. After he'd left, the director was really angry, swearing under his breath and slamming down papers as he worked.

NEIGHBOUR. He was angry at the man? Or himself?

CLEANER. Why would he be angry at himself? No, he was just angry. Then I thought he was talking to me, but they never do that, so he can't have been.

NEIGHBOUR. What did he say?

CLEANER. I wish I was washing those walls.

NEIGHBOUR. He must've been talking to you.

CLEANER. Do you think? Even though they aren't allowed. Maybe you're right, maybe he was.

Scene Two

Two men at a tea shop.

Pause.

THIEF 1. Tea?

THIEF 2. That's what we normally do here, isn't it?

THIEF 1. Yeah.

  Pause.

THIEF 2. So go on then.

THIEF 1. Go on what?

THIEF 2. Pour me some tea then.

THIEF 1. Sorry, here.

  THIEF 1 *pours* THIEF 2 *some tea. He hands it to him, and watches him while he sips it.*

THIEF 2. You poisoned it or something?

THIEF 1. Poisoned it? No, why would I, poisoned it? No. I would never do that.

THIEF 2. How touching.

THIEF 1. But I wouldn't.

THIEF 2. OK. Good. (*Pause.*) Aren't you having some?

THIEF 1. Yeah.

  He pours himself some tea but just holds it and doesn't drink.

  Pause.

THIEF 2. What's on your mind, sweetheart?

THIEF 1. Nothing. Princess.

THIEF 2. I'm not going to beg you like a woman, so if there is, / you better just

THIEF 1. OK. I just don't want you to think . . . look, I wouldn't poison you, OK? I wouldn't do that.

THIEF 2. No, yours is a less subtle form of violence.

THIEF 1. I'm not joking. You've taught me a lot, and

THIEF 2. Are you thanking me?

THIEF 1. No.

THIEF 2. Are you dying?

THIEF 1. Dying? No. Well, not imminently, to my knowledge.

THIEF 2. A relief to us all.

THIEF 1. No, I'm just, I'm, well. I want to go. Give this new capital a shot.

Silence.

THIEF 2. New capital, it's a dirt-track lay-by, there aren't even tea shops yet. Why would you go unless you were forced?

THIEF 1. New opportunities for one thing.

THIEF 2. We do alright here, don't we?

THIEF 1. Barely. Think of all those untapped sources, all those innocent country folk.

THIEF 2. They've got nothing worth stealing.

THIEF 1. And all those rich people who'll be moving there . . . they have nothing worth stealing either?

THIEF 2. This is my home.

THIEF 1. What difference does it make to you where we are? Home is any place there are people to provide for you.

THIEF 2. This is my home. I may not be winning any citizen of the year awards, but it's where I live. I could tell you where I was with my eyes shut.

THIEF 1. What good's that?

THIEF 2. You really think country living would suit you?

THIEF 1. It might.

THIEF 2. Well, I've got plenty to be getting on with here.

THIEF 1. Like what?

THIEF 2. Nothing, I'm sure, compared with your city of opportunity, but still, I'll manage.

THIEF 1. We're a team.

THIEF 2. Going to be pretty hard if you're out conning peasants in the middle of nowhere and I'm here, isn't it?

THIEF 1. You've got a plan, haven't you?

THIEF 2. If we're no longer partners, I think it would be short-sighted of me to discuss any prospects with you.

THIEF 1. Don't be like that, I haven't left yet, it's just an idea. We're still partners. You need me.

THIEF 2. I need you, do I?

THIEF 1. We need each other.

THIEF 2. I did fine before.

THIEF 1. But with me, you've done more than fine.

THIEF 2. Maybe. But don't think I need you. I'm happy to go back to fine.

THIEF 1. But why go back to that when . . . it's a whole new city / just waiting

THIEF 2. I don't want anything to do with it. It's a rat hole. People are only moving there because they have to. There's nothing there, it's a forgotten loggers' town, / you're mad

THIEF 1. There will be hundreds of thousands there soon, just think of all the opportunities.

THIEF 2. I'm staying.

THIEF 1. In this rat hole?

THIEF 2. At least I have the choice. Which is more than can be said for a lot of them.

THIEF 1. If you could make a real decision, would you, honestly, choose to stay here? Would this place be your choice?

THIEF 2. Yes.

THIEF 1. They should employ you as an ambassador.

THIEF 2. I'd never work for them.

THIEF 1. I'm pretty sure you don't have to worry about that.

THIEF 2. I saw a man that does being escorted to a van, heading for the new capital. His new home, although I'm pretty sure he was happy with his old one. It was nice, just by the lake there, I was admiring it.

THIEF 1. I bet you were.

THIEF 2. A family too. They stood in the drive, watching him being led away.

THIEF 1. He left his wife alone?

THIEF 2. With the kids.

THIEF 1. Girls?

THIEF 2. Two boys. The youngest was crying, but he must've been ten.

THIEF 1. Mummy's boy.

THIEF 2. She held him. The other one, he couldn't hold it together either, he ran after his father, hugging him and gripping him tight. Please don't go. Please don't go.

THIEF 1. But he went?

THIEF 2. He didn't have a lot of choice.

THIEF 1. He left them all alone?

THIEF 2. There are probably servants, house like that.

THIEF 1. Is this part of your plan, boss?

THIEF 2. I'm just telling you what I saw.

THIEF 1. Where is this house?

THIEF 2. But you go. I'll be just fine.

THIEF 1. Don't be like that. There's always time for a
profitable job.

THIEF 2. That your groundbreaking business theory, is it?

Pause.

THIEF 1. Tea, boss?

THIEF 2. No.

THIEF 1. I might just . . .

THIEF 1 *pours himself more tea and sips it slowly.*

There were no daughters, you say?

THIEF 2. Not that I saw.

THIEF 1. Still, the wife was attractive?

THIEF 2. The house was attractive.

THIEF 1. There are probably hundreds of men like him, right?
Spineless civil servants, lapdogs at the feet of the man in
charge, abandoning their homes and their loved ones.

THIEF 2. I think abandoning is a little / strong

THIEF 1. What would you say?

THIEF 2. His head was bowed. A cold sweat was dripping off
him. He was escorted by two other men.

THIEF 1. He didn't have to leave. He doesn't have to do what
he does.

THIEF 2. It didn't look like he was calling many of the shots.

THIEF 1. I know how that feels.

THIEF 2. Well, leave then.

Pause.

Look, they'll join him at some point, and that's our chance. What do you think?

THIEF 1. We don't need to wait that long.

THIEF 2. In a couple of months hundreds of houses will be empty. Sitting ducks, it's too easy.

THIEF 1. Why wait that long? A couple of months, where does that leave us now?

THIEF 2. Be patient.

THIEF 1. No. There are more opportunities if we move now.

THIEF 2. What kind of opportunities?

THIEF 1. It's your grand plan.

THIEF 2. Yes, it is.

THIEF 1. So you tell me.

THIEF 2. I have. We wait.

THIEF 1. Why can't you, for once, just . . .

THIEF 2. Just what?

THIEF 1. Just imagine. I keep thinking about that man's lonely wife. Abandoned. Vulnerable.

Pause.

THIEF 2. No. No. No. We don't do that.

THIEF 1. Why not?

THIEF 2. Why not? Because, because it's

THIEF 1. You've got to be open to new opportunities that present themselves. Times change, boss.

THIEF 2. Times change, yes, but that doesn't mean that you can . . . You're not going near her.

THIEF 1. Why not? Her husband clearly doesn't care, if he did he wouldn't have left.

THIEF 2. That's not a reason to

THIEF 1. Then why not?

THIEF 2. It's just an excuse.

THIEF 1. Why not? Just say it, go on.

THIEF 2. Because. Because it's

THIEF 1. Say it.

THIEF 2. It's . . . it's wrong.

> THIEF 1 *laughs*.

THIEF 1. Do you see? Can you hear how pathetic it sounds?

THIEF 2. Just go. Leave if you want to leave.

THIEF 1. But you've been kind enough to point out what I'd be missing here.

THIEF 2. It's not what I meant.

THIEF 1. We're friends.

> THIEF 2 *shakes his head*.

> Are we friends?

THIEF 2. Not if you do this.

> THIEF 1 *laughs*.

> What are you laughing at? Stop laughing.

THIEF 1. Do you think I haven't done this before?

> *Pause*.

THIEF 2. When?

THIEF 1. Are you kidding?

THIEF 2. When?

THIEF 1. I thought you just turned a blind eye.

THIEF 2. We just steal *things*, jewellery and / things

THIEF 1. Yeah, I've just stolen a few extras along the way. (*Laughs*.)

THIEF 2. When I've been there?

THIEF 1. What's that matter?

THIEF 2. On our jobs?

THIEF 1. Don't tell me you didn't know. You knew.

Silence.

Are you annoyed I didn't share?

THIEF 2. You're sick.

THIEF 1. What? You only rob them blind so you're OK? You knew. How could you not know?

THIEF 2. Just go. They're welcome to you in that rat hole.

THIEF 1. After I've finished up here I will.

THIEF 2. You're not going in that house.

THIEF 1. Really?

THIEF 2. I won't let you do that.

THIEF 1. You let me before.

THIEF 2. I didn't let you, I would never have . . .

Pause.

Please. Just leave them.

THIEF 1. Stop pretending you didn't know, be honest for once. I know you, you must've seen something special in that house and you want it for yourself.

THIEF 2. Just leave them.

THIEF 2 *squares up to* THIEF 1, *who laughs and pushes him back*.

THIEF 1. You can't tell me what to do, boss. You're stuck here, and what's worse, you're happy about it. But I'm getting out. I won't miss these opportunities.

THIEF 2. Opportunities?

THIEF 1. Yes. Opportunities.

THIEF 2. I won't let you near that house.

THIEF 1. I'm not asking you.

> THIEF 1 *goes to leave*. THIEF 2 *gets in his way*.

THIEF 2. No.

THIEF 1. No what?

THIEF 2. No.

> *In his effort to leave*, THIEF 1 *punches* THIEF 2, *who falls to the ground*.
>
> THIEF 1 *exits*.

Scene Three

Afternoon. Two CIVIL SERVANTS *sit outside*. CIVIL SERVANT 2 *is sewing a button onto one of his shirts*.

CIVIL SERVANT 1. I refuse to do that.

CIVIL SERVANT 2. Sew a button on?

CIVIL SERVANT 1. I just buy a new shirt.

CIVIL SERVANT 2. Seems a bit extreme.

CIVIL SERVANT 1. Ah, but once things start going wrong with it, a button here, a sleeve there, you might as well just call it a day. Move on.

CIVIL SERVANT 2. When has your sleeve ever fallen off?

CIVIL SERVANT 1. I've got one at the moment that's ripped at the seam, actually, on the shoulder.

CIVIL SERVANT 2. How'd you do that?

CIVIL SERVANT 1. It's poor quality, that's the problem. Not that it was cheap.

> *Pause*.

You know, I bet he doesn't have to sew his own buttons on.

CIVIL SERVANT 2. No?

CIVIL SERVANT 1. No.

CIVIL SERVANT 2. Who does sew them on?

CIVIL SERVANT 1. She probably does. In fact, yes, of course she does. Definitely. Why him? That's what I want to know. We're all staying here, but we, the unmarried, are snubbed. It doesn't make sense. The amount he sweats I bet he gets through a fair few shirts too, so why him?

CIVIL SERVANT 2. What've his buttons got?

CIVIL SERVANT 1. Exactly, what've his buttons got? He's married, he's already got a wife to sew his buttons on.

CIVIL SERVANT 2. Although, she's not here though, is she.

CIVIL SERVANT 1. That's not the point.

CIVIL SERVANT 2. No.

CIVIL SERVANT 1. He's already got sons to rip the buttons off, as they clamber over him, rolling around the manicured lawn in domestic bliss.

CIVIL SERVANT 2. Quite a picture.

CIVIL SERVANT 1. And all I have is new shirts.

Pause.

CIVIL SERVANT 2. If you want, if it's the buttons that bother you, I don't mind sewing them on for you.

CIVIL SERVANT 1. It's not the buttons.

CIVIL SERVANT 2. She might not even sew them on. We haven't seen her doing it.

CIVIL SERVANT 1. No, but have you seen the looks?

CIVIL SERVANT 2. What looks?

CIVIL SERVANT 1. She smiles at him.

CIVIL SERVANT 2. Maybe.

CIVIL SERVANT 1. And he smiles back.

CIVIL SERVANT 2. Do you want me to smile at you?

CIVIL SERVANT 1. You?

CIVIL SERVANT 2. Well, yes.

CIVIL SERVANT 1. I don't think it would help.

CIVIL SERVANT 2. Sure.

> CIVIL SERVANT 2 *smiles anyway.* CIVIL SERVANT 1
> *looks at him unimpressed.*

Sorry.

CIVIL SERVANT 1. She doesn't smile at us.

CIVIL SERVANT 2. She might be busy.

CIVIL SERVANT 1. Yeah, busy with him.

CIVIL SERVANT 2. And her husband.

CIVIL SERVANT 1. The poor man.

CIVIL SERVANT 2. It's just a smile.

CIVIL SERVANT 1. There's no such thing as just a smile.

CIVIL SERVANT 2. But he seems to miss his wife and children.

CIVIL SERVANT 1. All the more reason he would try to satisfy his longings, with whoever's to hand.

CIVIL SERVANT 2. You think he'd do that?

CIVIL SERVANT 1. It's what he's done.

CIVIL SERVANT 2. I think he's just . . . friendly.

CIVIL SERVANT 1. Have you seen him at the table? He eats all the crap she serves. All of it. That's more than friendly. Why would he force himself to eat some peasant mush unless he was accepting other favours?

CIVIL SERVANT 2. Maybe he's hungry?

CIVIL SERVANT 1. Why are you defending him?

CIVIL SERVANT 2. I didn't know it was a trial.

CIVIL SERVANT 1. It's not a trial. We're just two guys having a chat. But you seem to want to contradict me at every opportunity. Why is that?

CIVIL SERVANT 2. I don't.

CIVIL SERVANT 1. There you go again. You sit there. Sewing.

CIVIL SERVANT 2. My button fell off.

CIVIL SERVANT 1. And you have the gall to defend this adulterous man.

CIVIL SERVANT 2. You don't know that.

CIVIL SERVANT 1. I've just heard you.

CIVIL SERVANT 2. You don't know that he's adulterous.

CIVIL SERVANT 1. He certainly sweats like he's got something to hide.

CIVIL SERVANT 2. A few smiles and a healthy appetite aren't enough / to condemn

CIVIL SERVANT 1. Are you in on it?

CIVIL SERVANT 2. In on it?

CIVIL SERVANT 1. This scheme they've got going.

CIVIL SERVANT 2. I've lost you, I'm afraid.

CIVIL SERVANT 1. You can't afford to do that.

Silence.

CIVIL SERVANT 2. Look, I don't want to get into any . . . I'm not sure, I . . . Look, yes, they like each other. I thought it was innocent. But maybe, maybe it's not. You could be right, I mean, what does a smile really mean?

CIVIL SERVANT 1. Now you're talking.

CIVIL SERVANT 2. And why would she have cause to smile?

CIVIL SERVANT 1. Exactly. Unless . . .

CIVIL SERVANT 2. Unless, yes, exactly.

CIVIL SERVANT 1. And you know he's being considered for promotion?

CIVIL SERVANT 2. Promotion?

CIVIL SERVANT 1. Yes. He does nothing but pine for home all day, and his name's on the list.

CIVIL SERVANT 2. That's not fair.

CIVIL SERVANT 1. You don't need to convince me. You know, the amount he sweats, he probably drinks twice as much as the rest of us.

CIVIL SERVANT 2. Twice as much?

CIVIL SERVANT 1. Maybe more. And I don't need to tell you, there's hardly an endless supply.

CIVIL SERVANT 2. An adulterous husband, with an insatiable thirst, who makes a cuckold of his host. He's the man they promote?

CIVIL SERVANT 1. It's not definite yet.

CIVIL SERVANT 2. Do you know if . . . am I on the list?

CIVIL SERVANT 1. I don't . . . Probably not. In fact, no.

CIVIL SERVANT 2. But our buttons are coming off, your seam was ripped, in the line of duty, and what's he care? He's got someone to sew them back on.

CIVIL SERVANT 1. You see what I'm talking about now.

CIVIL SERVANT 2. I smiled at him.

CIVIL SERVANT 1. I know.

CIVIL SERVANT 2. His wife was probably happy to see him go if this is how he behaves.

CIVIL SERVANT 1. Yeah, she deserves a real man. Have you seen her?

CIVIL SERVANT 2. No.

CIVIL SERVANT 1. You want to.

CIVIL SERVANT 1 *smiles at* CIVIL SERVANT 2, *who smiles back.*

Pause.

When you smiled at him, I wasn't sure if . . . if you were with him.

CIVIL SERVANT 2. I was never with him.

CIVIL SERVANT 1. But you did smile at him, you said so yourself.

CIVIL SERVANT 2. Well, yes, but only in a natural way, it was more of a twitch than anything else.

CIVIL SERVANT 1. You were trembling maybe?

CIVIL SERVANT 2. Yes, it was more a quiver, than a smile.

CIVIL SERVANT 1. You were smiling because you were scared.

CIVIL SERVANT 2. Exactly. I was scared. It wasn't a smile, I was trembling.

CIVIL SERVANT 1. It doesn't make much sense to smile because you're scared.

CIVIL SERVANT 2. It was a knee-jerk reaction, I'd say.

CIVIL SERVANT 1. One you wouldn't repeat?

CIVIL SERVANT 2. Not now, no.

CIVIL SERVANT 1. Because, you have to be careful. Like earlier, offering to smile at me . . .

CIVIL SERVANT 2. Was stupid, I know.

CIVIL SERVANT 1. Even after I'd said not to.

CIVIL SERVANT 2. I'm sorry.

CIVIL SERVANT 1. Enough. How's that shirt coming along?

CIVIL SERVANT 2. Almost there, I think.

CIVIL SERVANT 1. You must be more careful with your buttons.

CIVIL SERVANT 2. I will be.

CIVIL SERVANT 1. So you're almost done with your shirt.

CIVIL SERVANT 2. Yes.

Pause.

I'm sorry, would you like me to do your sleeve for you?

CIVIL SERVANT 1. I thought you'd never ask.

He smiles.

Scene Four

ENTREPRENEUR *and* CARPENTER *are working on the interior of a new tea shop.*

ENTREPRENEUR. And I've ordered some red plastic chairs. For outside.

CARPENTER. Yeah, that's great.

ENTREPRENEUR. I thought the red would stand out, grab attention.

CARPENTER. Great.

ENTREPRENEUR. You don't think blue is better?

CARPENTER. No. I always want to sit down when I see red chairs.

ENTREPRENEUR. Good. Well, I've ordered them now.

CARPENTER. You can always paint them.

ENTREPRENEUR. Do you think I should?

CARPENTER. No, but if you change your mind, you can.

ENTREPRENEUR. Nice to have the choice, is that what you mean?

CARPENTER. Exactly. You wake up one morning and think, my chairs should be blue, they can be blue. Simple as that.

Now how do you want this counter finished? Do you want me to varnish it?

ENTREPRENEUR. Do you think I should?

CARPENTER. It depends on the look you're going for.

ENTREPRENEUR. I trust you. Do what you think's best.

CARPENTER. But it's your shop.

ENTREPRENEUR. I trust you.

CARPENTER. I can't make all the decisions for you, you're an entrepreneur now, you got this place, / you're going to have to

ENTREPRENEUR. You haven't made all the decisions. I ordered the chairs, didn't I?

CARPENTER. Yes, you did.

ENTREPRENEUR. OK, so, you haven't made all the decisions. And sorry if I just want to involve my friends, I didn't know it was such a burden / on you

CARPENTER. OK. OK. I'll varnish it.

ENTREPRENEUR. If you think.

CARPENTER. Yes. I think.

ENTREPRENEUR. Well, do it now, it'll look better in the photos.

CARPENTER. What photos?

ENTREPRENEUR. Didn't I tell you?

CARPENTER. What photos?

ENTREPRENEUR. The ones she'll take. She said she'd be here early afternoon.

CARPENTER. Oh right.

ENTREPRENEUR. I don't know where she'll want me to pose, but, if it looks good, I could stand in front of the counter.

CARPENTER. Be careful not to stick to it.

ENTREPRENEUR. Yeah, that'd be embarrassing!

CARPENTER. Sure would.

ENTREPRENEUR. It's a shame the chairs haven't arrived yet, they might've looked good, I could've sat in one. For the photo.

CARPENTER. I'm sure she'll understand.

ENTREPRENEUR. Yes, she sounded understanding.

CARPENTER. That's good.

ENTREPRENEUR. In fact, she sounded very nice.

CARPENTER. Do you want a coloured varnish?

ENTREPRENEUR. I don't mind. You know, she called me.

CARPENTER. I'll do a dark tint, that'll look smart.

ENTREPRENEUR. I've never had a journalist call me before.

CARPENTER. You've never been of use to one before!

ENTREPRENEUR. It's surprising the benefits having a tea shop brings.

CARPENTER. Maybe she's a friend of your new comrades.

ENTREPRENEUR. Maybe.

CARPENTER. They probably put her on to you. Bit of publicity, makes them look better if you do well, doesn't it.

ENTREPRENEUR. I hadn't thought about it.

CARPENTER. Well, you should. They still staying with you?

ENTREPRENEUR. They're with us indefinitely.

CARPENTER. Trouble alright?

ENTREPRENEUR. Why wouldn't she be?

CARPENTER. Well, it's more work for her, isn't it? Washing, cooking. It's alright for you as far as I can see, you've got a tea shop out of it, but she's the one that has all the extra work.

ENTREPRENEUR. I've earned this tea shop. My home's been invaded for the past two months. I get served last at my own table. We have to smile at these men, and we have no choice. I've paid for this tea shop.

CARPENTER. But that man, the one with the clammy handshake, he got the money for you.

ENTREPRENEUR. It's a government grant, anyone could've applied for it. You could've, but you / didn't.

CARPENTER. They hardly advertised them.

ENTREPRENEUR. They were open to everyone.

CARPENTER. Then how come you got one?

Silence.

ENTREPRENEUR. Are you not happy for me?

CARPENTER. Yes, of course I'm, I'm happy.

ENTREPRENEUR. I want you to be part of this, I need you.

CARPENTER. Of course I'm happy for you.

ENTREPRENEUR. I don't know what I'm doing, how to do this, this business, the dealings.

CARPENTER. You're doing fine.

ENTREPRENEUR. I'm not.

CARPENTER. It opens tomorrow, of course you're doing fine. Another lick of varnish and you're there. I'm proud of you, I mean, obviously you couldn't have done it without me, but, you know that.

ENTREPRENEUR. Like you said, I don't know why I got the grant. There must've been better candidates. I didn't know, what he wanted me to do, so I

CARPENTER. What did you do?

ENTREPRENEUR. After I . . . after I said it, he was shaking with anger, actually shaking.

CARPENTER. What did you say?

ENTREPRENEUR. I offered him, I offered her, to him.

Silence.

CARPENTER. Your wife?

ENTREPRENEUR. I offered

CARPENTER. You said those words? You were able to say those words?

ENTREPRENEUR. I thought it's what he wanted.

CARPENTER. And her? You think that's what she wanted? Your wife.

ENTREPRENEUR. No, well, I don't know. They smile at each other sometimes, and I thought, he got me this grant, so

CARPENTER. They smile at each other?

ENTREPRENEUR. He was really angry. I'm a family man. I have a wife and sons, and you think that's what I want? Is that what you think of me?

CARPENTER. Even if that is what he wanted, you can't just come out with things like that. Of course he was fucking angry.

ENTREPRENEUR. Is that what you think of me? He really wanted to know.

CARPENTER. You offered her. To him.

ENTREPRENEUR. I didn't want to.

Pause.

CARPENTER. I can't sleep any more. Do you know why? Because of the lights. With the new electric system the lights stay on all day and night. Why they need to be on in the day I don't know, but nonetheless, twenty-four hours a day, every day, they shine away. My neighbour has a new motorbike too, which he likes to rev all night. He used to have a bicycle, but I don't know, maybe he offered his wife to the nearest official and all of a sudden this shining red monstrosity sits outside his house. The revving doesn't help, but I could block that out if it wasn't for the lights.

ENTREPRENEUR. I could buy you a blind.

CARPENTER. I could buy myself a bloody blind.

ENTREPRENEUR. Well, why don't you then?

JOURNALIST *enters the tea shop*.

JOURNALIST. Wow, this is great.

ENTREPRENEUR. You're here. Come in.

CARPENTER. She has already.

JOURNALIST. The opening's tomorrow, isn't it?

ENTREPRENEUR. Yes. Tomorrow. It's just the finishing touches at the moment. Last few coats of varnish, that kind of thing.

JOURNALIST. You must be very proud.

Pause.

ENTREPRENEUR. Can I get you a cup of tea? My special recipe.

CARPENTER. My mother gave it to you.

JOURNALIST. A traditional recipe? Really? You should sell it as that. That's great. (*Makes notes*.) Local secret recipe.

ENTREPRENEUR. Yes, I suppose it is.

JOURNALIST. We're concerned to show traditions aren't being lost.

CARPENTER. Of course you are.

JOURNALIST (*to* CARPENTER). I'm sorry, I didn't know anyone else was going to be here.

ENTREPRENEUR. He's a friend.

CARPENTER. I'm just the carpenter.

ENTREPRENEUR. And an old friend.

JOURNALIST. You worked on the shop?

CARPENTER. Yes.

JOURNALIST. Well, congratulations, it looks great.

ENTREPRENEUR. He's not trained as a carpenter, but we've been friends for years, and this is a family enterprise, so . . .

CARPENTER. A family enterprise!

JOURNALIST. You're not trained? Really? Well, that just goes to show, doesn't it? What we can achieve, the potential we've all started to realise in ourselves, since, since all this began. It's amazing.

ENTREPRENEUR. He was a logger, so he's always worked with wood, haven't you?

CARPENTER. It's not quite the same now.

JOURNALIST. Exactly, that's what I'm saying. It's the same, but not the same, it's better.

ENTREPRENEUR. I've always wanted to get into business.

CARPENTER *laughs*.

JOURNALIST. And now you've been given the opportunity. Fantastic. What line of business were you in before?

CARPENTER. Logging.

JOURNALIST. Logging? That's great, a real rural job. My family were all loggers too.

ENTREPRENEUR. Well, I was more the management side of things.

CARPENTER. He was allowed to drive the lorry sometimes.

ENTREPRENEUR. There was more to it than that, obviously.

JOURNALIST (*laughs*). I can see you two get on well. You know what would be a fantastic shot, is the two of you. Two ex-loggers and look what they've achieved. I could have a front-page story on my hands.

CARPENTER. Tea shop opening? I'm sure there must be more pressing issues.

JOURNALIST. Ah, but it's what you make of these stories that counts. 'Tea Shop Opens' isn't immediately attention-grabbing, no, but it's what it represents.

CARPENTER. The only one in my family to have their picture taken was my uncle when he was imprisoned.

JOURNALIST. Well, this could be your lucky day!

CARPENTER. No.

JOURNALIST. You don't want to be in the photo?

CARPENTER. No. I don't.

ENTREPRENEUR. He's camera shy.

JOURNALIST. I think it could make the front page.

ENTREPRENEUR. Why don't we stand in front of the counter.

ENTREPRENEUR *moves towards it,* CARPENTER *doesn't.*

(*To* CARPENTER.) Can you just . . . for the photo.

JOURNALIST (*to* CARPENTER). It'd be quite a shot. The two of you.

CARPENTER. No.

JOURNALIST. I have got to get to an interview over at the new hotel, so I can't wait forever.

ENTREPRENEUR. The new hotel, great. (*To* CARPENTER.) Just for the photo.

JOURNALIST. You should take a peek, it's quite something.

CARPENTER. They probably wouldn't let me in.

JOURNALIST. It's open to everyone.

Pause.

CARPENTER. I'll leave you to it.

JOURNALIST. OK, fine. (*To* ENTREPRENEUR.) If you could just stand against the counter.

ENTREPRENEUR *rather awkwardly poses in front of the counter*.

ENTREPRENEUR (*to* CARPENTER). Be in the photo with me.

CARPENTER. You're leaning against the wet varnish.

CARPENTER *leaves*. ENTREPRENEUR *jumps away from the counter; it is slightly sticky*.

ENTREPRENEUR. It's fine, we can redo it, I can get someone else to redo it.

JOURNALIST (*making more notes*). And all this was possible because of a government grant, is that correct?

ENTREPRENEUR. Yes, it is.

JOURNALIST. Fantastic. So it's fair to say, your dreams have come true. It's the stuff of Hollywood, isn't it? Your family must be so proud.

ENTREPRENEUR. Do you know when the article will go in?

JOURNALIST. Tomorrow, probably.

ENTREPRENEUR. That soon?

JOURNALIST. Oh yes, we can work day and night.

ENTREPRENEUR. Don't you sleep?

JOURNALIST (*laughs*). No time for that.

Scene Five

GIRL (*fourteen*) *and* BOY (*fifteen*) *are in the woods. He grabs her by the arm.*

GIRL. You're afraid of me, aren't you?

BOY. Why would I be afraid of you?

He leans forward and kisses her. She pulls away.

GIRL. No. That's what he said to her.

BOY. Was he big?

GIRL. Not as big as her husband. No, not really.

BOY. All those city lot are weedy. Was he wearing a gun?

GIRL. I don't think so.

BOY. I've heard they all do.

GIRL. Well, he wasn't. He wouldn't carry a gun.

BOY. Oh, you know him, do you?

GIRL. He speaks to me sometimes.

BOY. Why would he do that?

GIRL. The first time he asked me for a towel. He said he was
    hot, he was sweating loads, so I got him one.

BOY. He was hot?

GIRL. He said he just wasn't used to the heat. That he missed
    the breeze.

BOY. Weedy city boys. Don't know what hot is.

GIRL. He said, I reminded him of his boys.

BOY. You're a girl.

GIRL. He has a son my age.

BOY. You haven't mentioned him before.

GIRL. He's only spoken to me a few times.

BOY. Do you fancy him?

GIRL. No, that's not / what . . .

BOY. So stop going on about him.

GIRL. I'm not, I'm just telling you what I saw.

BOY. You shouldn't have been watching.

GIRL. She said she was. Afraid of him. And he let her go.

BOY. Do you like spying on people?

He pulls her nearer and tries to kiss her. She resists.

GIRL. I wasn't spying.

BOY. Do you like teasing people?

GIRL. When you smiled at me, were you scared of me?

BOY. No, I probably wanted you to kiss me.

He moves in. She resists.

GIRL. He kept asking her. When you smiled at me, were you scared of me? Over and over.

BOY. You just stood there watching this?

GIRL. I didn't want to move, in case they saw me.

BOY. What did she say?

GIRL. She nodded. But I know that's a lie.

BOY. Are you scared of me?

GIRL. I know that's a lie, because she's mentioned him to me. She wasn't always scared of him. She liked him. She said he had a nice smile.

BOY. Do you think I've got a nice smile?

BOY *smiles,* GIRL *nods and smiles.*

Well, there you go then, that's the important thing.

GIRL. He grabbed her and started kissing her.

BOY. Like this.

BOY *grabs her quickly and kisses her. She struggles out of his hold.*

GIRL. Stop it.

BOY. Is that what she said?

GIRL. No, she didn't do anything. He was kissing her, his hands were all over her body and she didn't do anything.

BOY. I'm getting the feeling she wasn't up for it.

GIRL. Then he stopped.

Silence.

I'm getting my own office, with hard marble walls and floors, and a cleaner who won't be allowed to talk to me, and if I talk to her, she'll assume it's because I want something.

Pause.

He was crying.

BOY. The man's crying because he's got his own office and someone to clean it?

GIRL. I think he was crying because she wouldn't talk to him.

BOY. Personally I think talking gets a bit boring after a while.

GIRL. I want to tell you what I saw.

BOY. Why? It's some woman you help with the washing and a weedy city man crying about his office.

GIRL. He grabbed her, holding her close, and then started pulling her clothes off.

BOY. Now you get to the point.

GIRL. I should've gone in, said something. He wouldn't have done it if he'd seen me.

BOY. He would've. Maybe not then, but he would've.

GIRL. No. I know he wouldn't.

BOY. How do you know that? What? He's spoken to you so he must be alright? He probably doesn't even have kids. That's his chat-up line, but unfortunately for him, he didn't know that it takes a lot more than that to get anywhere with you!

GIRL. He does have kids, he has a son my age.

BOY. So what if he does, he was still ripping clothes off the woman who does his washing.

GIRL. Is this what you think of me? he was shouting.

BOY. He's scum, that's what I think of him.

Pause.

Come here.

He puts his arms around her. They stand for a moment.

GIRL. She was naked.

Pause.

And he started to rub himself against her. His belt buckle was grinding into her. He was moaning.

Pause.

And hard.

BOY *moves away.*

BOY. I don't want to hear this.

GIRL. Why not?

BOY. You shouldn't have been watching.

GIRL. He undid his trousers.

BOY. Why are you telling / me this?

GIRL. He forced himself inside her. Then he grunted and released her.

Silence.

BOY. This kind of thing . . .

GIRL. Get dressed. He did up his trousers but she didn't move. Get dressed I said.

BOY. It shouldn't be like that. It doesn't have to be.

GIRL. He was picking up her clothes and throwing them at her. But they just fell to the floor again.

Pause.

BOY. Look. You like those new jeans you bought, don't you?

GIRL. I can't believe / you.

BOY. You do though. You look good in them and you know it.

GIRL. You bought new jeans too, and those shirts.

BOY. I know. And I like them. I like that we can buy them. And lots of things have changed. My aunt's got a job at that new hotel. We've got new school buildings. There's more people, it feels like the place is alive now.

GIRL. So?

BOY. So that man brought those things with him.

GIRL. He didn't even want to come. He wanted to go home, he told me.

BOY. Well, he should've.

GIRL. Just before he left her, he said, 'He did offer.'

BOY. What's that supposed to mean?

GIRL. I don't know.

BOY. I'm sorry you had to see this, beautiful.

GIRL. She sat down, holding her head in her hands for a minute or two. Not long. Then she picked up her clothes, got dressed and went about her business. That was it.

BOY. She knows.

GIRL. What does she know?

BOY. She just knows. It's a kind of sacrifice.

GIRL. I could've helped him.

BOY. Him? I don't get you. Why would you help that scum?

Pause.

GIRL. I liked him. I could've stopped him.

BOY. You liked him? Is that what it takes? I knew you fancied him. After what he's done?

GIRL. I'm not saying what he did was right.

BOY. You better not be.

GIRL. I'm not. It wasn't.

BOY. Am I not man enough for you?

GIRL. You're not a man yet.

BOY. You think I'm a kid? If you need me to prove . . .

He starts to unbutton his trousers.

GIRL. I don't need you to prove it.

BOY. Obviously you do. You think I'm a weed?

He grabs her.

GIRL. No. You're very strong.

BOY. Am I?

GIRL. Yes. Very strong.

GIRL smiles.

Scene Six

WOMAN *and* DRIVER *sit next to each other at the front of* DRIVER*'s moving cart. He holds the horse reins.*

Silence.

DRIVER. Did you think you could walk the whole way?

Pause.

You know it takes nine hours? And that's by cart.

Pause.

Although it's getting faster. Some sections of the road have already been done, and they say the journey will be three hours when they've finished. Imagine that. A third of the time.

Pause.

That's in a car though, I suppose it'll still take six hours or so for me. That's if they let me on their new roads. If not, I'll have to take the back roads, and it'll probably take me longer than before. Never mind. I think I prefer the rocky paths we had anyway, they were so uncomfortable it kept me awake at least. The smooth roads can be a little hypnotic.

Pause.

It's nice to have someone to talk to.

Silence.

My daughter says I can talk the hind legs off a donkey . . . that's how I lost the last one actually, old Lightning.

WOMAN *gives him the faintest recognition.*

You're not staying for the parade then?

WOMAN. I wouldn't stay if he begged me.

DRIVER. Oh.

WOMAN. If he thinks I was going to stay there

DRIVER. You didn't like the place?

WOMAN. I despise the place.

DRIVER. Well, you wouldn't have liked it much before, then.

Pause.

How long were you there?

WOMAN. Too long.

DRIVER. You have to give these things time, it might've grown on you.

WOMAN. You make it sound like a fungus. I don't want anything growing on me.

DRIVER. I only meant you might grow to like it.

WOMAN. I won't.

Pause.

DRIVER. It'll be a show no doubt. All the uniforms and marching, I'm sure it'll be a grand display. I wanted to go but there's too much work at the moment. I've never been.

Pause.

WOMAN. You aren't missing much.

DRIVER. You've been?

WOMAN. I'm expected to cheer.

DRIVER. Should you be there tomorrow?

WOMAN. That's my husband's problem. He'll have to explain that.

DRIVER. So he works for the authorities?

WOMAN. Yes.

Silence.

Coward.

DRIVER. Are you calling me a coward?

WOMAN. Him.

DRIVER. Because I'd remind you, you are on my cart.

He slows the cart slightly.

WOMAN. Him. My husband.

He allows the cart to resume its normal pace.

DRIVER. I take it you're travelling to the old capital?

WOMAN *nods.*

You live alone while your husband is away?

WOMAN. No. I'm not alone.

DRIVER. You have children then?

WOMAN. Sons.

DRIVER. Good, you are protected.

WOMAN. They're only young.

DRIVER. Still, a son's instinct is always to protect his mother.

WOMAN. But if they aren't strong enough

DRIVER. They better hope they have a strong mother!

Pause.

WOMAN. Or that their father comes home.

Silence.

DRIVER. You can't move to be with your husband? I hear they've almost finished the accommodation, heard it's impressive.

WOMAN. Move to that place?

DRIVER. Perhaps he'll return to you then?

WOMAN. He seems to have settled in there.

DRIVER. It just takes a bit of time. We can adapt to a new place very quickly, you know, and soon you forget.

WOMAN. Forget what? Who you are?

Pause.

Do you use the new name for your home?

DRIVER. I use Royal City, yes. Why not? I prefer to live in Royal City than in Fleeing Chicken. How could anyone take us seriously with a name like that?

WOMAN. Some are calling it Rat Hole. That's the one I use.

DRIVER. I'd say that was a dangerous thing to call it.

WOMAN. I'd say it's apt.

DRIVER. Did your husband really have to move to the Royal City?

WOMAN. It wasn't royal then, and yes, he did. He wasn't allowed to resign.

DRIVER. Is this just what he told you?

WOMAN. You think he wanted to leave his wife and two young sons to camp out in some peasant's hovel?

DRIVER. The authorities didn't think it was a hovel.

WOMAN. Of course they did, and that's why it's perfect for them. Somewhere as shit-infested as them, where they can blend into the surroundings, where the flies are distracted by other equally foul-smelling things. It's a perfect rat hole, they've moved somewhere so repulsive no one will dare follow them, unless they're forced. They can get on with whatever obscene acts they want because the people here can no longer tell one kind of shit from another. A good man doesn't stand a chance.

DRIVER. Do you want to walk?

WOMAN. I was happy walking, yes. As long as I'm moving away from that place, I'm satisfied.

DRIVER. Then walk. I don't have to listen to this.

DRIVER *slows the cart. When it stops* WOMAN *gets down.*

Pause.

Neither the cart nor WOMAN *move.*

WOMAN. The road is long.

DRIVER. It is. Nine hours. By cart.

WOMAN. And the path isn't as safe as it once was.

DRIVER. There is certainly more traffic now.

WOMAN. And I need to see my sons.

DRIVER. I'm sure they want to see you.

WOMAN. I need to see my sons.

DRIVER. I'm not stopping you from seeing them.

WOMAN. I need to.

DRIVER. You wanted to walk.

WOMAN. I have to see them, to know I'm not crazy, to know that what I remember having, what I'm grieving for, did, once, exist. Because you're right. In that place, you do forget.

DRIVER. So walk.

WOMAN. Please. I need to get back.

Pause.

DRIVER. You can get back on, if you promise not to damn my home.

WOMAN. Don't make me promise.

DRIVER. It's only a short way, you can't even bite your
tongue for that distance? I bet you've got your husband into
some trouble in the past, haven't you?

Pause.

WOMAN. Please.

DRIVER *eventually nods and* WOMAN *climbs back onto
the cart. They continue on in silence for a while.*

DRIVER. He did the journey in eight-and-a-half hours one
time, you know. Old Lightning.

Pause.

It might not seem fast now, but, well, we were the talk of
the town for a while. Some of them tried to claim, there
was talk of steroids and such, but they just couldn't accept
that . . .

Pause.

No, I didn't drug him, I just whipped him 'til he bled.

WOMAN *looks at him.*

Only kidding, I sang to him. Honestly, it always gave him
an extra spring in his step. My daughter says he was just
trying to escape my dulcet tones. Well, I don't know, but it
always worked.

WOMAN. I didn't leave, my husband asked me to go.

DRIVER. Oh.

WOMAN. He begged me to. I was holding onto him, trying to
breathe him in. Then he pushed me away, he's never done
that. If he thinks he's protecting me somehow . . . he's not.
I grabbed him again, and for a moment, a moment, he let
me hold him. I could taste his sweat. But then he fell to his
knees. He was on his knees, he had his arms around my
waist, and he begged me to go.

Silence. The cart continues to carry them forward.

A Nick Hern Book

The Eleventh Capital first published in Great Britain as a paperback original in 2007 by Nick Hern Books Limited, 14 Larden Road, London W3 7ST in association with the Royal Court Theatre, London

The Eleventh Capital copyright © 2007 Alexandra Wood

Alexandra Wood has asserted her right to be identified as the author of this work

Cover image: © iStockphoto.com/Harry Ogloff
Cover design: Ned Hoste, 2H

Typeset by Country Setting, Kingsdown, Kent CT14 8ES
Printed in Great Britain by Bookmarque, Croydon, Surrey

A CIP catalogue record for this book is available from the British Library

ISBN 978 1 85459 988 9